Starting with... Role play

Colour and light

Diana Bentley
Maggie Hutchings
Dee Reid

Diana Bentley is an educational consultant for primary literacy and has written extensively for both teachers and children. She worked for many years in the Centre for the Teaching of Reading at Reading University and then became a Senior Lecturer in Primary English at Oxford Brookes University. Throughout her professional life she has continued to work in schools and teach children aged from 5 to 11 years.

Maggie Hutchings has considerable experience teaching KS1 and Early Years. She is a Leading Teacher for literacy in The Foundation Stage and is a Foundation Stage and Art coordinator. Maggie is passionate about the importance of learning through play and that learning should be an exciting and fun experience for young children. Her school's art work has been exhibited in The National Gallery, London.

Dee Reid is a former teacher who has been an independent consultant in primary literacy for over 20 years in many local authorities. She is consultant to 'Catch Up' – a special needs literacy intervention programme used in over 4,000 schools in the UK. She is Series Consultant to 'Storyworlds' (Heinemann) and her recent publications include Think About It (Nelson Thornes) and Literacy World (Heinemann).

Other titles in the series:

Ourselves
At the shops
Into space
Emergency 999
At the hospital
Fairytales
At the garage/airport
All creatures great and small
On the farm
Water
Colour and light

Other Foundation titles:

Starting with stories and poems:

    Self esteem
    Self care
    A sense of community
    Making relationships
    Behaviour and self control

    A collection of stories and poems

Starting with our bodies and movement

Starting with sounds and letters

The authors would like to thank Jane Whitwell for all her hard work in compiling the resources and poems for the series.

Published by
Hopscotch Educational Publishing Ltd, Unit 2, The Old Brushworks, 56 Pickwick Road, Corsham, Wiltshire, SN13 9BX
Tel: 01249 701701

© 2006 Hopscotch Educational Publishing

Written by Diana Bentley, Maggie Hutchings and Dee Reid
Series design by Blade Communications
Cover illustration by Sami Sweeten
Illustrated by Susan Hutchison
Printed by Colorman (Ireland) Ltd

ISBN 1 905390 12 2

Diana Bentley, Maggie Hutchings and Dee Reid hereby assert their moral right to be identified as the authors of this work in accordance with the Copyright, Designs and Patents Act, 1988.

The authors and publisher would like to thank Chapter One (a specialist children's bookshop) in Wokingham for all their help and support. Email: chapteronebookshop@yahoo.co.uk

All rights reserved. This book is sold subject to the condition that it shall not, by way of trade or otherwise, be lent, hired out or otherwise circulated without the publisher's prior consent in any form of binding or cover other than that in which it is published and without a similar condition, including this condition, being imposed upon the subsequent purchaser.

No part of this publication may be reproduced, stored in a retrieval system, or transmitted, in any form or by any means, electronic, mechanical, photocopying, recording or otherwise, without the prior permission of the publisher, except where photocopying for educational purposes within the school or other educational establishment that has purchased this book is expressly permitted in the text.

Starting with role play – Colour and light

Contents

Introduction	4
'Colour and light' planning chart	6
Week 1 – Celebrating Diwali	7
Week 2 – Making rainbow colours	11
Week 3 – More rainbow colours	14
Week 4 – Finding out about light	18
Week 5 – Exploring colours	21
Week 6 – Mixing colours	24
Photocopiables	27

Acknowledgements

'Diwali Morning' by Jill Bennett, from *Collections: Early Years Poems and Rhymes* compiled by Jill Bennett, 1993, published by Scholastic.
'November the Fifth' by Wendy Lamont. © Wendy Lamont. Reproduced by kind permission of the author.
'Bonfire Night' by Irene Yates. © Irene Yates. Reproduced by kind permission of the author.
'Mixing Colours' by Eric Finney. © Eric Finney. Reproduced by kind permission of the author.

Every effort has been made to trace the owners of copyright of material in this book and the publisher apologises for any inadvertent omissions. Any persons claiming copyright for any material should contact the publisher who will be happy to pay the permission fees agreed between them and who will amend the information in this book on any subsequent reprint.

Introduction

There are 12 books in the series **Starting with role play** offering a complete curriculum for the early years.

Ourselves	At the garage/At the airport
Into space	Emergency 999
At the shops	All creatures great and small
Colour and light	Under the ground
At the hospital	Fairytales
On the farm	Water

While each topic is presented as a six-week unit of work, it can easily be adapted to run for fewer weeks if necessary. The themes have been carefully selected to appeal to boys and girls and to a range of cultural groups.

Each unit addresses all six areas of learning outlined in the *Curriculum Guidance for the Foundation Stage* and the specific Early Learning Goal is identified for each activity and indicated by this symbol.

Generally, differentiation is achieved by outcome although for some of the Communication, Language and Literacy strands and Mathematical Development strands, extension activities are suggested for older or more confident learners.

Suggested teaching sequence for each unit

Each week has been organised into a suggested teaching sequence. However, each activity in an area of learning links to other activities and there will be overlap as groups engage with the tasks.

The Core Curriculum: Literacy and Mathematics

Every school will have its own programmes for literacy and mathematics and it is not intended that the activities in the units in this book should replace these. Rather, the activities suggested aim to support any programme, to help to consolidate the learning and to demonstrate how the learning can be used in practical situations.

The importance of role play

'Children try out their most recent learning, skills and competences when they play. They seem to celebrate what they know.'

Tina Bruce (2001) Learning Through Play: Babies, Toddlers and the Foundation Years. London: Hodder & Stoughton.

Early years practitioners are aware of the importance of play as a vehicle for learning. When this play is carefully structured and managed then the learning opportunities are greatly increased. Adult participation can be the catalyst for children's imaginations and creativity.

Six weeks allows for a role play area to be created, developed and expanded and is an optimum time for inspiring children and holding their interest. It is important not to be too prescriptive in the role play area. Teachers should allow for children's ideas and interests to evolve and allow time for the children to explore and absorb information. Sometimes, the children will take the topic off at a tangent or go into much greater depth than expected or even imagined.

Organising the classroom

The role play area could be created by partitioning off a corner of the classroom with ceiling drapes, an old-style clothes-horse, chairs, boxes, large-scale construction blocks (for example, 'Quadro') or even an open-fronted beach tent/shelter. Alternatively, the whole classroom could be dedicated to the role play theme.

Involving parents and carers

Encourage the children to talk about the topic and what they are learning with their parents or carers at home. With adult help and supervision, they can explore the internet and search for pictures in magazines and books. This enriches the learning taking place in the classroom.

Outside activities

The outdoor classroom should be an extension of the indoor classroom and it should support and enhance the activities offered inside. Boys, in particular, often feel less restricted in outdoor play. They may use language more purposefully and may even engage more willingly in reading and writing activities. In the

Introduction

outdoor area things can be done on a much bigger, bolder and noisier scale and this may connect with boys' preferred learning styles.

Observation in Salford schools and settings noted that boys access books much more readily when there is a book area outdoors.

Resources

Role play areas can be more convincing reconstructions when they are stocked with authentic items. Car boot sales, jumble sales and charity shops are good sources of artefacts. It is a good idea to inform parents and carers of topics well in advance so they can be looking out for objects and materials that will enhance the role play area.

Reading

Every week there should be a range of opportunities for children to participate in reading experiences. These should include:

Shared reading

The practitioner should read aloud to the children from Big Books, modelling the reading process; for example, from left to right along the lines of print and from the top of the page to the bottom. Shared reading also enables the practitioner to draw attention to high frequency words, the spelling patterns of different words and punctuation. Where appropriate, the practitioner should cover words and ask the children to guess which word would make sense in the context. This could also link with phonic work where the children could predict the word based on seeing the initial phoneme. Multiple readings of the same text enable them to become familiar with story language and tune in to the way written language is organised into sentences.

Independent reading

As children become more confident with the written word they should be encouraged to recognise high frequency words. Practitioners should draw attention to these words during shared reading and shared writing. Children should have the opportunity to read these words in context and to play word matching and word recognition games. Encourage the children to use their ability to hear the sounds at various points in words and to use their knowledge of those phonemes to decode simple words.

Writing

Shared writing

Writing opportunities should include teacher demonstration, teacher scribing, copy writing and independent writing. (Suggestions for incorporating shared writing are given each week.)

Emergent writing

The role play area should provide ample opportunities for children to write purposefully, linking their writing with the task in hand. These meaningful writing opportunities help children to understand more about the writing process and to seek to communicate in writing. Children's emergent writing should occur alongside their increasing awareness of the 'correct' form of spellings. In the example below, the child is beginning to have an understanding of letter shapes as well as the need to write from left to right.

Assessment

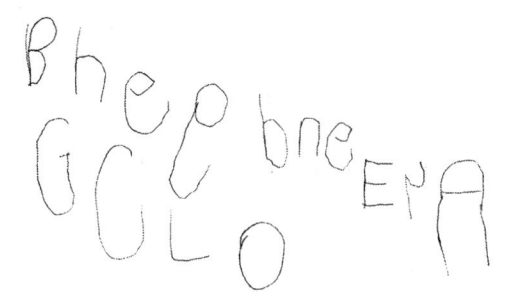

When children are actively engaged in the role play area this offers ample opportunities for practitioners to undertake assessments. By participating in the role play area the practitioner can take time to talk in role to the children about their work and assess their performance. The assessment grid on page 35 enables practitioners to record progress through the appropriate Stepping Stone or Early Learning Goal.

DfES publications

The following publications will be useful:

Progression in Phonics (DfES 0178/2000)
Developing Early Writing (DfES 0055/2001)
Playing with Sounds (DfES 0280/2004)

'Colour and light' planning chart

Colour and light	Role play area	Personal, Social and Emotional Development	Communication, Language and Literacy	Knowledge and Understanding of the World	Mathematical Development	Creative Development	Physical Development
Week 1	This is a home celebrating Diwali	Have a developing respect for own cultures and others. Discussing celebrations Talking about safety with candles	Listen to and use spoken and written language Telling story of Rama and Sita Phonics – d, f, l, c Making recipe cards	Observe features of the place where they live Exploring how candles burn Decorating divas Tasting Diwali food	Use language to compare quantities Using mathematical vocabulary for length and weight Using number line	Sing simple songs from memory Making Rangoli patterns Singing Diwali songs Making shadow puppets	Move with control and coordination Dancing to Indian music Making symmetrical patterns
Week 2	Visiting the rainbow house and discovering what colours it becomes	Respond to significant experiences Looking at homes and houses	Listen with enjoyment; respond to stories Sharing story Phonics – rhyming pairs Shared writing	Identify features of the natural world Looking at rainbows Naming colours Creating a rainbow	Count reliably up to ten Matching items to coloured box Addition of items Number sequence	Explore colour, shape and texture Making tissue flowers Making a village	Travel around, over, under, through Following instructions 'Stuck in the mud' 'Over and under'
Week 3	Decorating the rainbow house	Take turns, sharing fairly Discussing favourite colours Sequencing coloured beads with partner	Writing for different purposes Making simple books Reading colour poems Labelling colours	Look at similarities What colours are in the playground? Ask questions Making chart of different colours	Add and subtract Forming numbers correctly Counting the numbers on a dice	Explore colour Making mobiles, rainbow birds, rainbow chains Making a fireworks frieze	Use imagination in music and dance Moving to music and making shapes
Week 4	Entering the science laboratory and finding out about light	Be motivated to learn Discussing being curious, wanting to find out about things	Explore meanings and sounds of new words Introducing new vocabulary Phonics – forming cvc words Writing up investigation	Investigate objects, using senses Looking at manufactured and natural light	Use language of comparison Weighing on scales Discussing probability of quantity	Use imagination in art and design Making kaleidoscopes and periscopes	Move with control and coordination Children mirroring your movements Moving to music
Week 5	Exploring the colours of autumn	Show a range of feelings Discussing colours in environment Looking at jealousy through biblical story of Joseph	Sustain attentive listening Listening and responding to story Responding to poems Phonics – looking at further initial letter sounds	Identify features in natural world Looking at colours in autumn leaves Making a collage	Words to describe position Playing 'Hide the red brick' Colour sequencing with beads Number matching 1–5	Explore colour and shape in two dimensions Making camouflage pictures Colouring Joseph's coat	Move with control and coordination Following instructions on ways to move Dancing as a leaf in the wind
Week 6	Having a rainbow party	Understand codes of behaviour Taking turns, talking politely Looking at hygiene	Read a range of common words Making sets of high frequency words – children matching words Orally constructing sentences for writing	Identify objects they observe Creating coloured lenses Playing commercial 'colour' games	Addition and subtraction Using laying a table to support adding places and taking away places	Explore colour, shape, texture Exploring colour mixing Making rainbow biscuits and jellies	Show awareness of space Playing the colours game Moving to actions in a song

Colour and light

In this six-week unit, the children will be exploring many aspects of colour and light. Talk and play will revolve around the colours of the rainbow, growing things and houses and gardens. A central feature of the unit will be stories about the rainbow. In preparation for the unit, collect a range of shiny and/or reflective objects, such as mirrors, spoons, shiny paper and foil paper and containers.

At the end of the unit the children will have created a rainbow house and garden, and also have made:

- a display board with rainbow houses
- a rainbow mobile
- a rainbow bird
- Rangoli patterns
- a clay thumb pot for a diva
- a 'fireworks' picture
- rainbow biscuits and jellies

Dressing-up box

Resource the dressing-up box with suitable costumes – such as, Indian fabrics, junk jewellery, hats of the individual colours of the rainbow, ribbons in different colours, lab coats made from white shirts.

WEEK 1

Diwali: the Hindu festival of lights
(This week should coincide with the actual week of the festival.)

The role play area

This week the role play area will become a home celebrating Diwali. The children will be encouraged to dress up in Indian clothes and to eat some typical sweets eaten at a Diwali celebration. Under supervision the children will light the role play area with **candles** and place them in the **clay thumb pots** they have made. The class will be told the story of Rama and Sita and will make **shadow puppets** to help them to retell the story. They will also make **Rangoli patterns** and **wax resist pictures of Hanuman, Rama and Sita**.

Celebrating Diwali

Resources

Photocopiables:

Poems and songs 1 (page 27)
The story of Rama and Sita (page 29)
How to make barfi sweets (page 30)
Diva template and Rangoli designs (page 31)

Fiction books:

Rama and the Demon King by Jessica Souhami, Frances Lincoln (0 711211 58 2) (also available in big book format, 0 711214 48 4)
The Divali Small Book by Anita Ganeri, Evans (0 237524 71 6)
The Divali Big Book by Anita Ganeri, Evans (0 237524 69 4)

Non-fiction books:

My Divali by Monica Hughes, 'Little Nippers: Festivals' series, Heinemann Library (0 431186 36 7)
My Hindu Faith by Anita Ganeri, 'Red Rainbows' series, Evans (0 237518 96 1)
Oxford Literacy Web: First Words – Non-Fiction by Diana Bentley, Oxford University Press (0 199174 73 3)
Diwali by Chris Deshpande, A&C Black (0 713640 82 0)

Materials:

- Posters and pictures of Hindu temples
- Tea lights
- White household candles of varying sizes
- Self-hardening clay
- Stiff card
- Large cardboard box for puppet theatre
- Sticks – for example, thin garden cane for the shadow puppets
- Variety of fruits, including dried fruits, cut up into small portions and placed in small dishes

Music and songs:

CD of Indian music

Personal, Social and Emotional Development

Have a developing respect for their own cultures and beliefs and those of other people.

Festivals

❑ In circle time discuss different celebrations. Ask the children what they do when they celebrate their birthdays. Ask what other festivals they know (Christmas, Passover, Ramadan).

Safety

❑ Talk about the way we have to behave in order for everyone to be safe. Explain the need to look out for other people when you are holding a lighted candle (see Creative Development).

❑ Remind them to keep away from the hot lamp when they are showing their shadow puppets (see Creative Development). Discuss the way we should help other people to be aware of danger.

Communication, Language and Literacy

Enjoy listening to and using spoken and written language and readily turn to it in their play and learning.

Vocabulary extension

❑ During these sessions the children should become familiar with the following vocabulary: celebration, festival, fun, giving, gifts, sparkle, glitter. Encourage them to use the vocabulary in their conversations with adults.

Reading aloud

❑ Read the story of Rama and Sita from a story book (or use page 29) to the class. Discuss the story with the children.

Poems

❑ Read the Diwali poem on page 27. Talk about the poem and ask the children which words tell us it is about Diwali. Encourage them to join in with you as you say it.

Phonics

❑ Introduce initial phonemes, such as 'd' (Diwali), 'f' (festival), 'l' (light) and 'c' (candle). Use other words and ask the children to listen to the initial sound and then identify the phoneme.

❑ Play 'Spot the odd one out'. Ask the children to tell you the two words that start with the same sound from a list – for example, 'dog', 'Diwali', 'mouse'. Continue with other letters but revisit each letter at least three times. Have the letter written on a piece of card to help them link the letter sound with its graphic form.

Invisible writing

❑ Write a child's name, using a white household candle on white paper. Paint over with a wash to reveal the name.

Celebrating Diwali

Writing recipes

- Tell the children that they are going to make recipe cards for Diwali sweets. Talk about the purpose of a recipe (it explains what you need and how to make something). What do the children think the sweets are made from? Demonstrate writing a list of ingredients. Make cards for each of the ingredients and ask the children to choose some for their sweet. Give each child a blank card and tell them to write these as a list on it. Less confident writers could draw pictures of the ingredients. Demonstrate writing the method for making Diwali sweets (page 30).

Extension

- More confident writers could attempt to list the ingredients without copying the ingredients cards.

Mathematical Development

Use language such as 'greater' and 'smaller' to compare quantities.

Mathematical vocabulary

- Make a collection of candles of varying lengths. Ask the children to arrange them, starting with the shortest.
- Invite them to choose a candle and then find something longer or shorter. Challenge them to cut a strip of paper the same length as their candle and then to cut a piece of string the same length as their candle.
- Discuss the various widths of the candles. Ask them to show you the thickest, lightest, heaviest, thinnest, largest, smallest, longest and shortest.

Using a number line

- Ask the children to pick up six candles and show you where they would fit on the number line. Ask them how many would be left if you took away two candles.

Extension

- Demonstrate how to write this as a sum, 6 − 2 = 4. Do the same with addition. Encourage the children to use the vocabulary of 'more than' and 'less than'.

Counting in twos

- Put the candles in sets of two and talk about counting two at a time. Encourage the children to say '2, 4, 6, 8, 10'. Ask them to stand in twos, then fours, and invite another child to count them. Encourage them to write the numbers on their whiteboards.

Knowledge and Understanding of the World

Observe, find out about and identify features in the place where they live and in the natural world.

Exploring how candles burn

- Under careful supervision, light a candle and ask the children to observe what happens as it burns (it gives light and heat and the wax melts). Ask them which part of the candle is burning. Talk about the different parts of a candle (wax, wick, flame) and ask which part gives the light. Why do they think the flame moves? (The air above the candle is warm and warm air rises. Cold air is drawn in to take its place. This movement of air is why a candle flame flickers, although it could also be a draught in the classroom or the effect of the children breathing.)

Decorating divas

- Ask each child to draw a diva (traditional clay pot to hold a candle) and colour the pot and the flame. Alternatively, use the template on page 31. Display these in the role play area. If possible, show the class a real diva. Talk about how families would have many divas to light their homes.

Diwali food

- Light the divas the children made in Creative Development and compare this to lighting candles on a birthday cake. Create a festive atmosphere and have a selection of sweets (either buy or make barfi sweets on page 30) and nibbles (small pieces of banana, apple, apricot) prepared for Diwali celebrations. Note: be aware of sweets containing nuts.

Diwali clothes

- Look at pictures of a Diwali celebration (see Resources for non-fiction books). Ask the children what the people are wearing and whether we wear similar/different clothes. Talk about special clothes for special occasions.
- If possible, arrange for a visit by a member of the Hindu faith.

Starting with role play – Colour and light

Celebrating Diwali

Creative Development
Sing simple songs from memory.

Singing songs
- Sing a song for Diwali, such as 'Candles glowing' (page 27).

Making divas
- Talk to the class about divas, their purpose and appearance. Make divas, using salt dough (2 cups plain flour, 1 cup salt, 1 cup water, bake until hard) or clay. Have a tea light or small candle as a guide to size and shape. When dry or baked, decorate the pots with brightly coloured paints. The children could add glitter, sequins or other shiny objects.

Rangoli patterns
- Explain that these symmetrical patterns are created at the front door as a welcome or greeting to guests. Show the children the Rangoli patterns on page 31. Explain that they are often made with rice. Talk about the detail and symmetry of the patterns. Help them to create their own Rangoli patterns. They should draw a simple symmetrical pattern and fill it with rice, pulses or small pasta shapes.

Shadow puppets
- Help the children to draw images from the story of Rama and Sita on stiff card. Help them to cut out the images and attach them to the tips of garden canes. Invite them to retell the story on the wall in the role play area using their puppets and a lamp.

Puppet theatre
- Make a puppet theatre from a large box. Tape several layers of good quality tracing paper over the screen area. (Alternatively, cover a hinged clothes airer with white sheeting.) Invite the children to help you tell the story of Rama and Sita, moving the puppets accordingly.

Wax resist pictures
- Make wax resist pictures of the story of Rama and Sita. Tell the children to draw pictures from the story. using wax crayons on good quality paper. Explain that they need to press firmly and to make their pictures as colourful as possible. Make up a wash of very thin watercolour paint and water and let them paint over their pictures. What happens? Why do they think the paint only covers the paper and not the crayon?

Physical Development
Move with control and coordination.

Fine motor control
- Cutting out figures of Rama and Sita in Creative Development.

Moving to music
- Play a suitable record of Indian music. Explain how the movements in Indian dance are very carefully controlled. Show the children a simple hand movement and ask them to copy you. Then sway with the hips and ask the class to do the same. Move in time to the music. Finally, move slowly around the hall and tell the children to do the same as you.

Symmetrical patterns
- In pairs, one child draws a simple shape with his or her foot – for example, a semicircle. The partner then draws the other half – its mirror image.

Colour and light

WEEK 2

The role play area

This week the role play area will become the rainbow house. Each day the children will go into the house and see what colour it has become. On Monday the walls and furnishings will be red, Tuesday – orange, Wednesday – yellow, Thursday – green, Friday – blue. The progress through the rainbow colours will be concluded on Monday of Week 3 of the unit when the children will explore the colour purple. As they enter the rainbow house they should sing the rainbow house song (page 28). As each colour is introduced this should be charted in a large arc on the classroom wall, which will build to create a **rainbow**. The children will make a **rainbow village** with coloured doors and **paper flowers**.

Resources

Photocopiable:

Poems and songs 2 (page 28)

Fiction books:

At the End of the Rainbow by A H Benjamin, Little Tiger Press (1 845060 02 4)
Ned's Rainbow by Melanie Walsh, Dorling Kindersley (0 751372 67 6)
Duckie's Rainbow by Frances Barry, Walker Books (0 744596 46 7)
Mrs Rainbow by Neil Griffiths, Storysack (0 953709 91 4)
Stan's Rainbow Surprise by Debbie Foster, 'Hullabaloo Zoo' series, Brimax children's Books (1 858542 73 1)

Non-fiction books:

Colourful Days, Dorling Kindersley Readers (0 751343 97 8)

Music and songs:

Bobby Shaftoe Clap Your Hands by Sue Nicholls, A&C Black (0 713635 56 8)
The Handy Band by Sue Nicholls, A&C Black (0 713668 97 0)

Materials:

- Large paintbrushes
- Small buckets of water
- Assortment of small objects in each colour
- Tissue paper in each of the rainbow colours
- Shallow container (Pyrex pie dish)
- Mirror
- Sticky tack
- Torch
- Skipping ropes
- Range of photos/pictures of different houses
- Five 'posting' boxes covered with red, orange, yellow, green and blue paper
- Playground chalks

Making rainbow colours

Communication, Language and Literacy
Listen with enjoyment and respond to stories and rhymes.

The rainbow house
- Start the day by singing the rainbow house song (page 28) with the whole class. Reveal the colour of the day. Take groups of children into the rainbow house. Sing the rainbow song as you go in.
- Place a plastic crate of items in each of the colours outside the house. Children should select items that match the colour of the house that day and explain to you what they have selected – for example, 'I have chosen a red brick.'

Shared writing
- Write for the children each day 'Today our rainbow house is (red).' Write the sentence in the correct colour. Talk about where to start the writing, spaces between words and so on.

Rhyming pairs
- Play rhyming games based on the colour of the day. Ask the children if the following words rhyme – for example, 'red', 'bed'. (NB: for the 'orange' day suggest nonsense words such as 'porange', 'torange' and 'borange'.)

Extension
- Introduce rhyming pairs with an 'odd one out' – for example, 'red', 'fed', 'car'. Ask the children to identify the rhymes and non-rhymes.

Reading
- Read a story about the rainbow – for example, one of the stories from Resources. If possible, read this many times during the week and encourage the children to join in with you as you read.
- Look at a non-fiction book linked to the topic (see Resources) and talk about the colours. Leave the books accessible for the children to 'read' or browse through.

Songs
- Sing together the song 'Our street' in *The Handy Band* (see Resources).

Creative Development
Explore colour, texture, shape, form and space in two dimensions.

Exploring colour
- After the children have visited the house each day, they should paint, colour or cut out shapes in the colour of the day. These should be displayed on strips of colour.

Making paper flowers
- Cut out some petal shapes in different colours. Help the children to make large paper flowers. Tell them to scrunch up coloured tissue paper for the centre. Stick them on garden sticks and display on the classroom walls.

Making a rainbow village
- Make a template of a simple outline of a house on a piece of A5 paper. Ask the children to trace round the template and to colour the door the same as their own front door. Then they should cut round one side and the top of the door so that it opens. Arrange the houses with their coloured doors in a frieze to make a 'village'.

Outside activities
- Give the children large paintbrushes and small buckets of water. Encourage them to 'paint' flowers on the playground or walls. Discuss drying and absorbency.

Knowledge and Understanding of the World
Observe, find out about and identify features in the natural world.

Exploring rainbows
- Look at pictures of rainbows. If possible, observe actual rainbows. Discuss when rainbows appear in the sky. (Light is made up of all seven colours but we do not see them. When the sun is shining and it is also raining, the sunshine on the raindrops splits light into its separate colours.) Name the colours of the rainbow. (Use the mnemonic 'Richard Of York Gave Battle In Vain' to remember the sequence of the colours of the rainbow.)

Making rainbow colours

Creating a rainbow

❑ You will need a shallow container, a mirror, water, sticky tack, a torch and a sheet of white paper. Fix the mirror at an angle (sloping back) at one end of the dish. Half fill the dish with water. Shine the torch onto the submerged section of the mirror. Hold the paper above the torch. A rainbow will appear on the paper.

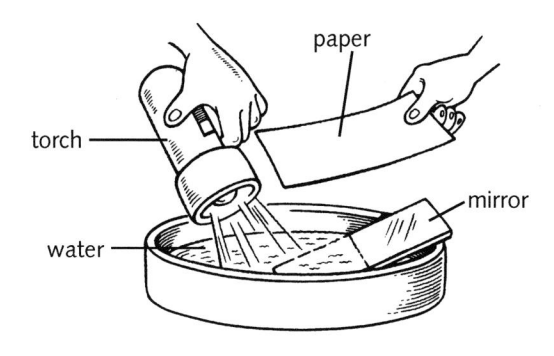

Personal, Social and Emotional Development

Respond to significant experiences.

Houses and homes

❑ Talk about the role play rainbow house. Ask the children what colour their front door is. Talk about what kind of house they live in and what makes their home comfortable and a place they like to live.

❑ Provide a collection of photos or pictures of various house styles and different environments – for example, village, town, city, countryside. Laminate the pictures and leave them out for the children to explore and discuss further.

Mathematical Development

Count reliably up to 10.

Colour and number matching

❑ Provide five boxes covered with appropriate coloured paper (red, orange, yellow, green and blue). Cut a 'posting hole' in each box. Provide children with a range of items in the five colours. Challenge the children to post the correct number of items in each box – for example, to put four red counters in the red box.

Extension

❑ Tell one child to put a number of items in the box and then a second child to put a further number in the same box. Ask: How many items are in the box now? Ask the children to write a sum to represent the numbers – for example, 3 + 2 = 5.

Number sequence

❑ Number the houses in the village picture (see Creative Development). If the display is at child level, put sticky tack on the back of each number and challenge the children to position the numbers in the correct order.

Extension

❑ With more able children, look at odd and even numbers. Demonstrate and explore odd and even numbers with Unifix.

❑ If possible, take a group of children to a street to observe how houses are really numbered.

Physical Development

Travel around, under, over and through.

Following instructions

❑ Draw houses, with chalk, on the playground. Encourage the children to move to the houses in different ways – for example, hop, skip, run, tiptoe, bounce, backwards, forwards, sideways.

Playground games

❑ Play the game 'Stuck in the mud'. Select one child to be the rain, another to be the sun. The rest of the children run around within a specified area. If caught by the rain, children must stand still, arms and legs outstretched, until released by the sun. The sun 'frees' children by crawling through their legs.

❑ Play the game 'Over and under'. Pairs of children form an arch with their arms or a bridge using a rope on the ground. Other children see how many arches they can go under and how many bridges they can go over before you call 'Stop'.

Colour and light

WEEK 3

Activities for bonfire night are included in this week.

The role play area

This week the children will complete the colours of the rainbow. On Monday the walls and furnishings will be purple (combining indigo and violet) and the purple band should also be added to the large rainbow arc on the classroom wall. Children will also be making **rainbow mobiles** and **paper chains** in rainbow colours to decorate the role play area and **rainbow birds** to live in the rainbow garden.

Resources

Photocopiables:

Poems and songs 2 (page 28)
Rainbow mobile (page 32)

Fiction books:

Where Are You, Blue Kangaroo? by Emma Chichester-Clark, HarperCollins (0 007109 96 2)
Brown Bear, Brown Bear, What Do You See? by Bill Martin, Puffin (0 140502 96 3)
Duckie's Rainbow by Frances Barry, Walker Books (0 744596 46 7)
Rainbow Fish by Marcus Pfister, North-South Books (1 558584 41 2)

Non-fiction books:

Weather by S Matthews, 'First Discovery' series, Moonlight Publishing (1 851030 85 9)
Why Can't I Slide Down a Rainbow? by Sally Hewitt, Belitha Press (1 841384 43 7)

Music:

'The Four Seasons' by Vivaldi, (or other weather music for dancing)

'Fireworks Music' by Handel

Materials:

- Clipboards
- Shop-bought bubble mix
- Variety of sizes and shapes of bubble rings
- Assortment of objects in each colour – for example, building bricks, plastic toys
- Lightweight blue card
- Circle of white paper for the sun
- Old CDs
- Shiny paper
- Decorative glass stones
- Cotton wool
- Glue sticks
- Gummed paper in a variety of colours
- Coloured string
- Corks
- Coloured feathers
- Coloured beads and laces
- Pack of paper chains
- Sticky tack

Games:

Commercial colour and shape games – for example, Colour dominoes or Knickerbocker Glory (GLS – www.glsed.co.uk)

More rainbow colours

Personal, Social and Emotional Development

Work as part of a group, taking turns and sharing fairly.

Explaining preferences

❑ In the role play area, ask groups of children to discuss which is their favourite colour. From a box of objects of many colours, invite them to select something in their favourite colour and describe it to the others.

Threading beads

❑ Organise the children into pairs. Provide each pair with strings and coloured beads. Tell them to recreate the sequence of the rainbow colours as depicted in the rainbow on the classroom wall. They should negotiate and discuss which colour follows which.

Fireworks

❑ Ask them what they have seen or think they will see at a fireworks display. Ask questions such as: What did you notice about the rockets? What happened to the sparkles before they went out? (They started to fall to earth.) Why must we be careful when there are fireworks about? How should we keep safe?

Communication, Language and Literacy

Writing for different purposes.

Phonics

❑ Label the colours of the large class rainbow. Write the following letters on cards and use sticky tack to fix these to the whiteboard; 'r', 'o', 'y', 'g', 'b', 'i', 'v'. Ask the children to tell you which letter you will need for the first letter in each colour. Ask individual children to select the letter and, if possible, write the first letter for you.

Independent writing

❑ Give each child a sheet of A4 paper. Ask them to choose a rainbow colour and draw something that colour. Using highlighter writing, model for them how to write: This _____ is _____. (This car is red.) Ask them to write inside the highlighter writing. Organise the pictures in the sequence of the colours of the rainbow and display them in a scrapbook.

Extension

❑ Encourage more confident writers to write their own captions for the book.

Listening

❑ Read the colour poems (see page 28) throughout the week and invite the children to learn some by heart. They could perform them to the class or in a school assembly.

❑ Share books about rainbows (fiction and non-fiction).

❑ Read a poem about bonfire night (see page 27). Encourage the children to say the poem with you.

Mathematical Development

Adding and subtracting.

Rainbow numbers

❑ Draw the outline of numbers 1–5, each filling a separate A4 sheet. Indicate with a dot the starting point for forming the number and use an arrow to indicate the direction. Demonstrate how to write the number inside the outline, using a red felt-tipped pen. Invite the children to add the other rainbow colours so that each outline is filled with the seven colours of the rainbow.

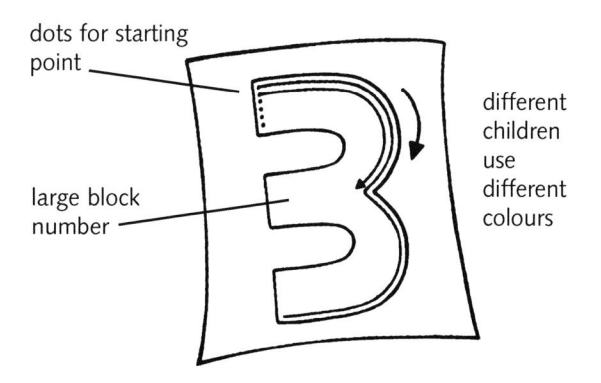

dots for starting point

large block number

different children use different colours

Dice game

❑ Tell the children to take it in turns to roll the dice. Then they should count the dots and write the numeral on their boards.

More rainbow colours

Extension
- Children take it in turns to throw the dice. They should record the number and then write the plus sign; for example, 4 +. They should throw again and fill in the number to complete the sum. Tell them to pass the sum to the next child and challenge them to do the addition. Can they roll two dice and challenge a partner to take the lower number from the higher?

Knowledge and Understanding of the World

Look closely at similarities, differences, patterns and change. Ask questions about why things happen and how things work.

Observing colours
- Ask the children to tell you what colours they can see in the playground and which colour they can see more than any other. Ask them to tell you how many different shades of a colour they can see – for example, green.
- Give the children clipboards with different coloured squares drawn down the side of a piece of paper. Ask them to put a tick beside each colour when they see a different object in that colour. At the end of the exercise, ask them which colour has the most ticks.
- The children could repeat this activity at home or they could draw pictures of the different objects they have at home for each colour.

Outdoor activity
- Provide bubble liquid (washing-up liquid and water, or a shop-bought mixture). Provide a range of sizes and shapes of bubble rings. Give the children the opportunity to investigate bubbles and encourage them to talk about their findings. Ask: Why did the bubble pop? What colours could you see? Could you see through the bubbles? Did the bubbles have the same colours as you can see in the rainbow?

Creative Development

Exploring colour.

Making the sun and rain
- Cut out a large circular sun and ask the children to help you print on the colour, using corks and orange paint. Place this near the class rainbow.
- Decorate the role play area with CDs or shiny paper raindrops and suspend them from the ceiling in front of the rainbow as raindrops. More raindrops could be made by sticking decorative glass stones onto strips of ribbon and suspending them from the ceiling.

Rainbow mobiles
- Use page 32 to make rainbow mobiles (you might like to enlarge it). Cut small squares of gummed paper the colours of the rainbow and small triangles of orange paper for the sun's rays. Store them in different trays. Help the children to cut out their rainbow, cloud and sun. They should stick the small squares of paper (in the correct colour order) onto both sides of their rainbow. Then they should glue cotton wool on to the cloud shape. They should colour the sun orange and then add the triangles of orange paper around the edge to represent the sun's rays. Fix the sun and cloud to the ends of the rainbow. Suspend with thread from the ceiling to make the mobile.

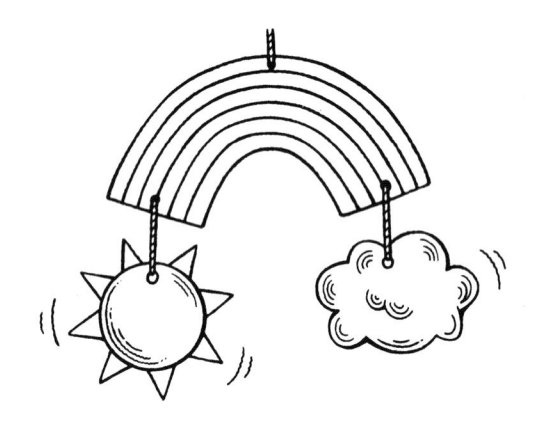

More rainbow colours

Rainbow bird

❑ Demonstrate how to create a rainbow bird (see diagram). Provide old CDs for the bird's body, coloured card circles for the eyes and feathers for the tail. Make a beak by cutting a small square out of the card and folding it in half. Make a small slit in the fold and show the children how to push this onto the CD. Cut legs and feet out of brown card. Now ask the children to use the resources to make their own. Thread ribbon, thin string or sewing thread through the hole in the centre of the CDs and suspend them from the ceiling in the role play area.

Rainbow chains

❑ Using paper chains, make a rainbow decoration for the rainbow house.

Extension

❑ Ask more able children to make a paper chain, following a pattern of colours – for example, 3 x blue; 3 x red; 3 x yellow.

Making a fireworks picture

❑ Use sheets of black sugar paper glued together to make a long frieze. Give the children reflective, shiny, glittery materials for their picture. Draw some items in glue for the children to sprinkle glitter over. Talk about the shapes and colours of the fireworks. Encourage the children to decide where to position different aspects of the scene.

Physical Development
Use imagination in music and dance.

Making rainbow shapes

❑ Ask the children to use their hands and feet to make a rainbow shape. Encourage pairs of children to make the arc of a rainbow by joining hands in an arch and leaning together.

Moving to music

❑ Using a short extract from Vivaldi's 'Four Seasons', or other suitable music, ask two children to form an arch and the other children to dance through the 'rainbow'. Encourage them to listen to the music, decide what kind of weather it depicts and dance accordingly.

Using a range of construction kits

❑ Using Lego or wooden bricks, make models of the rainbow village.

Interpreting music

❑ Explore the movement of fireworks – fast, zooming, spinning, turning, exploding and changing direction. If possible, perform to Handel's 'Fireworks Music'.

Starting with role play – Colour and light

Colour and light

WEEK 4

The role play area

This week the role play area becomes a 'science laboratory'. Make a **sign** for the role play area titled '**Laboratory**'. The children will become scientists finding out about light and shadows. They are going to look at light and experiment with making rainbows and mirror images. They will make **kaleidoscopes** and **periscopes** and use them in their investigations.

Resources

Photocopiables:

Poems and songs 1 and 2 (pages 27 and 28)
Template for making a periscope (page 33)
Template for making a kaleidoscope (page 34)

Fiction book:

Moonbear's Shadow by Frank Asch, Aladdin Paperbacks (0 689835 19 1)

Non-fiction books:

Taking Turns, by Janine Amos, 'Growing Up' series, Evans (1 842340 09 3)
Are Lemons Blue?, 'My First Book' series, Dorling Kindersley (1 405302 20 8)
Science Directions by Alison Norman, 'Early Years Big Book' series, Collins (0 003172 41 4)
Living with Light by N Baxter, 'Toppers' series Franklin Watts (0 749641 49 5)
Light and Dark by Claire Llewellyn, 'Start-up Science' series, Evans (0 237525 91 7)

Music and songs:

The Handy Band by Sue Nicholls, A&C Black (0 713668 97 0)

Materials:

- Sets of balancing scales
- Selection of objects for weighing, for example, corks
- Uniform size bottle tops; for example, cola tops
- Feathers
- Marbles
- Lolly sticks
- Small wooden blocks
- Matchsticks
- Lightweight balls (tennis ball size)
- Table tennis balls
- Empty cereal/food boxes
- Two mirrors the same size
- Three handbag-sized mirrors
- Coloured beads
- Spoons
- Shiny paper/foil
- Old white shirts (laboratory coats)
- Jam jar
- Button
- Torch
- Black sugar paper

18 **Starting** with role play – Colour and light

Finding out about light

Personal, Social and Emotional Development

Continue to be interested, excited and motivated to learn.

Circle time

❑ Talk to the children about being curious. What things would they like to know? Invite each of them to suggest a question starting 'Why …?' Model asking things they might wonder about – for example, 'I wonder why a rainbow has all those colours,', 'Why do trees grow so tall?' Go round the circle, asking the children to suggest a 'Why?' question. Talk about how asking questions helps us to learn.

❑ Talk about investigating and finding out. Explain that we need to look carefully/observe closely and talk about what we see. This makes us think about what might happen – for example, 'If I throw this ball up into the air, I think … might happen.' Remind the children about what they observed when they were watching the candle burn. What did they notice? What did they wonder about (why the flame moved)? What did they discover?

Taking turns

❑ Tell the children that they are going to be scientists this week and that they will be doing some experiments. They can wear laboratory coats (old white shirts) when they are investigating. Discuss how they need to take turns in trying things, listen to others and take turns in conversations and discussions.

Knowledge and Understanding of the World

Investigating objects and materials by using all of their senses as appropriate.

Exploring light and dark

❑ Talk to the children about light. If possible, darken the classroom. Ask them how you could make the classroom light again. Talk about the differences between manufactured light and natural light. Talk about why it is dark at night. Explain that the Sun is our main source of light and it is dark at night because there is no light from the Sun.

❑ Talk to the children about manufactured forms of light (light bulbs and candles). Light a candle and talk about how it gives light but not as much as a light bulb. Talk about all the different ways light bulbs are used (street lamps, Christmas lights, car headlights, flash cameras).

Reflected light

❑ In a dark room, shine a torch onto a mirror and direct the reflected light onto a shiny surface, such as a cupboard door. Explain that the torch is like the Sun and the mirror is like the Moon. The light from the mirror is just a reflection of the light from the torch, just as the light from the Moon is just a reflection of the light from the Sun.

Communication, Language and Literacy

Extending their vocabulary, exploring the meanings and sounds of new words.

Vocabulary extension

❑ Introduce the new vocabulary of the topic – for example, 'reflection', 'reflective', 'source', 'natural', 'manufactured'. Encourage the children to repeat and use this technical language.

❑ Read and share with the children a selection of non-fiction books about light (see Resources). Talk about the pictures and the information.

Phonics

❑ Say the word 'sun'. Separate it into phonemes s/u/n. Talk about the sound at the beginning – s. Extend the sound like the noise a snake might make. Write the grapheme 's' on the board. Ask the children what sound they can hear at the end of the word – n. Extend this sound – for example, 'nnnnnnnn'. Write this on the board, leaving a space for the vowel. Separate the phonemes and ask the children if they can hear the sound in the middle of the word 'sun'. Write this on the board. Explain that you are going to change the word from 'sun' to 'fun'. Ask them which phoneme has changed (the first one). Rub out 's' and replace it with 'f'.

Starting *with role play – Colour and light*   19

Finding out about light

Extension

- Give each child one of the phoneme cards 's', 'r', 'g', 'f' and 'b'. Go round the group and ask each child in turn to say the sound of 'their' phoneme. Write 'un' on the board. Tell the children you want to make the word 'run'. Whose phoneme card will make that word? Help the children to stick their card in place, using sticky tack. Continue with the remaining letters.

Shared writing

- Write a simple explanation for one of the investigations the children have explored – for example, the mirror box or the periscope. For example: 'We made a mirror box. We put one brick near the mirrors but we could see two bricks reflected in the mirrors.' Write the explanation on a large sheet of paper and display in the role play area.

Speaking and listening

- Talk about the investigations. Prompt responses with the questions: How many mirrors did we use? What did we see when we looked in the mirror? What could we do with the periscope? Which investigation did you like best?

Mathematical Development

Use language such as 'greater', 'smaller', 'heavier' or 'lighter' to compare quantities.

Weighing objects

- Using scales and a variety of objects, set tasks for the children to investigate in pairs or groups – for example:

    'I have put ten lolly sticks on one side of the scales. How many table tennis balls will I need to put on the other side to balance?'

    'I have put this big cereal box on one side of the balancing scales. How many marbles do you think I will need to put on the other side to balance?'

    Talk about things that are small and heavy or big and light. Which do the children think will be heavier – five feathers or five beads? Encourage them to talk about their findings with their partner or group. Record findings on paper – for example, five feathers (mini pictures) are lighter than five beads (mini pictures).

Extension

- Give pairs of children a collection of corks and bottle tops. Tell them to put five corks on one side of the balance and to predict how many bottle tops will be needed to balance the scales. When they have completed the experiment, give each pair drawings of balanced scales. Tell them to draw a cork and the number five on one side of the balance, and a bottle top and the correct number on the other side of the balance. Do the same with other items – for example, wooden blocks and tennis balls.

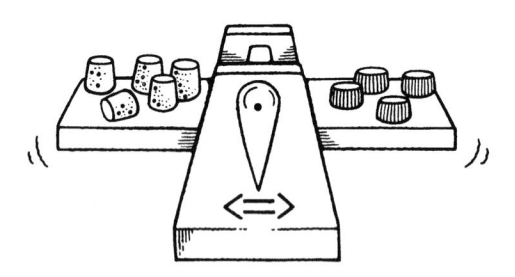

Creative Development

Use their imagination in art and design.

Light investigations

- Make the kaleidoscope and periscope (see pages 33 and 34). Talk to the children about what they can see. Give them time alone in the role play area so they can investigate further. Explore and investigate by putting objects in front of the mirrors. What can they see?
- On wet days, look at reflections in puddles.

Physical Development

Move with control and coordination.

Copying movements

- Tell the children that you are going to make a movement and they are to try to be like mirrors and do the same as you do. Gradually increase the complexity of the movements. Finally, ask the children to work with a partner to take it in turns to do a movement that their partner has to copy.

Colour and light

WEEK 5

The role play area

The next two weeks look at colour in the world, both manufactured and found in nature. The children think about the importance of colour and look at the various shades of each colour. The role play area will display the different colours that we find in nature. The children will learn about camouflage and will create **pictures of animals hidden in the environment**. They will also look at colours in nature (for example, **autumn leaves**) and make the role play area reflect the colours of autumn.

autumn leaves

pictures of animals hidden in the environment

Resources

Photocopiable:

Poems and songs 2 (page 28)

Fiction books:

Winnie the Witch by Valerie Thomas, Oxford University Press (0 192721 97 6)
Carlo Likes Colours by Jessica Spanyol, Walker Books (0 744598 31 1)
Elmer by David Mckee, Andersen Press (1 842703 45 5)
Joseph and His Amazing Coat by Heather Amery, Usborne Bible Tales (0 746054 33 5)
The Mixed-up Chameleon by Eric Carle, Puffin (0 140506 42 X)

Non-fiction books:

Colours by Robert Crowther, Walker Books (0 744575 49 4)
What Can You See? by Diana Bentley, Oxford Literacy Web: First Words – Non-Fiction, Oxford University Press (0 199174 73 3)

Amazing Colours by N Baxter, 'Toppers' series, Franklin Watts (0 749641 46 0)

Materials:

- Black and white photographs
- Coloured beads
- String
- Peg board
- Pegs
- Circles of different coloured paper (five colours)
- Marbling ink

Music and songs:

Songs from 'Joseph and the Amazing Technicolour Dreamcoat' (CD ASIN B000024H4E)

Starting with role play – Colour and light

Exploring colours

Personal, Social and Emotional Development

Respond to significant experiences, showing a range of feelings when appropriate.

Colours in the environment
- Talk to the class about colours they can see in the classroom and the playground. Ask them to tell you what colours they think the sky, sun, moon, trees and houses are. Ask: Do they ever change colour? What would our world be like if we couldn't see colours? If possible, show them black and white photographs and others in colour. Which do they prefer?

Joseph and his coloured coat
- Tell the class this story from the Bible. Talk about the brothers' feelings of jealousy and why they tried to get rid of Joseph.
- Invite the children to talk about the colours of their clothes. Ask them if they wear different clothes in summer and winter. Tell them that some colours are thought of as warm colours (reds, oranges, yellows) and some as cold colours (blues, greens).

Dressing up
- Ask some of the children to dress up in clothes from the dressing-up box and tell the class why they have chosen the clothes and what colours they have chosen.

Communication, Language and Literacy

Sustain attentive listening, responding to what they have heard by relevant comments, questions or actions.

Listening
- Read *Winnie the Witch* or *Elmer* to the class (see Resources). Spend time talking about the illustrations and the place of colour in the story. Invite the children to comment on the story.

Phonics
- Draw clear illustrations of people and things in the story; for example, Winnie – cat, tree, house or Elmer – elephant, tree, patchwork. Hold up the illustrations and ask the children to tell you the initial phonemes of the objects – for example, 'c' in cat, 'e' in elephant and 't' in tree.

Poetry
- Read the poem 'I like colours' on page 28. Draw the children's attention to the rhyming words. Generate more rhyming words; for example, sky, high – my, by, fly.

Mathematical Development

Use everyday words to describe position.

Language of position
- Play 'Hide the red brick'. Tell the children to work in pairs. Child A hides the brick in the role play area and then Child B searches for it. When it is found, Child B has to describe where he or she found it. Encourage the children to use the mathematical language of position (behind, in front of, inside, next to) to describe where the brick was hidden.

Colour sequencing
- Using either coloured beads and string or a peg board and pegs, create a pattern with a sequence of colours; for example, two red beads followed by two blue beads, followed by two red and so on. Ask the children what should come next in the pattern. Invite them to create a pattern for others to follow.

Exploring colours

Colour/number matching

- Write the numbers 1–5 on different coloured circles. Challenge the children to put items of the same colour and quantity by the correct circle – for example, four blue objects by the blue circle with number 4 on it.

Extension

- Ask the children to add the number of items on two circles and to represent this as a sum – for example, 2 + 3 = 5.

Knowledge and Understanding of the World

Observe, find out and identify features in the natural world.

Autumn

- Talk about the colours of the leaves on the trees and on the ground. Ask questions such as: What colour are leaves in the spring and summer? What colour are they in the autumn? What happens to trees in the autumn? If possible, take a short nature walk to collect a variety of fallen leaves. Draw three large outlines of leaves (for example, beech, oak, sycamore) on sugar paper. Ask the children to decide where each fallen leaf should be stuck to match the outline.
- Make a collage of leaves. Write a caption for the collage – for example, 'In autumn the leaves change colour and fall from the trees.' Display this in the role play area.

Creative Development

Explore colour, shape and form in two dimensions.

Camouflage

- Demonstrate how to colour a sheet of A4 paper, using marbling ink. Cut the coloured sheet into four. Keep two quarters for the background. On the back of the other two sections, draw or trace around a template of an animal such as a cat or snail. Cut the animals out and stick them onto the background. Encourage them to add details such as eyes or whiskers, beak and claws. Talk about how the animal is camouflaged. Why can't you see it easily? Look at examples of camouflaged animals in books (see Resources).

Colouring

- Draw a simple outline of Joseph's coat. Ask the children to colour it with rainbow colours.

Physical Development

Move with control and coordination.

Fine motor skills

- See Creative Development – cutting out animals for camouflage.

Movement and gymnastics

- Using suitable music, encourage the children to move around the hall like animals – for example, to slink like a cat, prowl like a lion, hop like a rabbit, jump like a kangaroo and crawl like a spider. Stop the music and tell the children to freeze in an animal shape.

Outdoor games

- Tell the children to pretend to be leaves attached to trees, moving gently in the wind. Then the wind gets stronger and the leaves fall from the trees and twirl down to the ground.

Starting with role play – Colour and light

Colour and light

WEEK 6

The role play area

This week the children will experiment with mixing primary colours to make a range of colours. The unit will end with a **rainbow party** where children will make **rainbow jellies**, decorate **rainbow biscuits** and drink fruit drinks in a variety of colours. They will write **invitations** and lay the table for the guests. If possible, encourage the children to come to the party wearing a jumper of their favourite colour.

(Illustration: children at a rainbow party with labels — invitations, rainbow biscuits, rainbow party, rainbow jelly)

Resources

Fiction books:

Lizzie's Invitation by Holly Keller, Walker (0 744513 92 8)
PB Bear's Birthday Party by Lee Davis, Dorling Kindersley (0 751350 72 9)
Grandpa's Handkerchief by Dorothy Clark, Hodder Children's Books (0 750007 84 2)
Mouse Paint by Ellen Stoll Walsh, Red Wagon Books (0 152002 65 0)
Anna's Amazing Multi-coloured Glasses by Wendy Body, Pelican Big Books, Longman (0 582333 48 2)

Non-fiction books:

White Rabbit's Colour book by Alan Baker, Kingfisher (1 856973 99 9)
No, Thank You! by Janine Amos, 'Good Manners' series, Evans (0 754090 23 X)
Wrong Colours by Dee Reid, Oxford Literacy Web: First Words – Non-Fiction, Oxford University Press (0 199174 78 4)
Mixing Colours – Red by Victoria Parker 'Little Nippers' series, Heinemann Library (0 431173 41 9)

Poems:

Red Rockets and Rainbow Jelly by Sue Heap and Nick Sharratt, Puffin (0 140567 85 2)

Websites:

www.bobthebuilder.org
www.kinderstart.com
www.dltk-kids.com

Games:

Any suitable commercial games to practise colour recognition – for example, 'Colour Clowns', 'Colour Paddles' or 'Knickerbocker Glory' (GLS – www.glsed.co.uk)

Materials:

- Strands of wool in various colours
- Cardboard tubes
- Coloured Cellophane
- Jam jars
- Writing icing (or icing sugar and food colouring)
- Cake decorations such as hundreds and thousands
- Fruit squash of different flavours – for example, orange, lemon, blackcurrant, cranberry, lime
- Straws of different colours
- Paper plates
- Plastic spoons
- Clear containers
- Jelly (red, green, yellow, blackcurrant)
- Rich tea biscuits
- Thin white card for invitations
- Plastic food

Mixing colours

Personal, Social and Emotional Development

Understanding that there need to be agreed values and codes of behaviour.

Personal hygiene
- Talk to the children about washing their hands before handling food and eating. Explain that bacteria are on our hands and only thorough washing with soap and water will ensure the germs do not get onto food.

Circle time
- Sit the children in a circle. Ask each child in turn if they would like to eat something. Suggest 'nice' things – for example, 'Would you like an apple?' They must answer 'Yes, please,' or 'No, thank you.' Suggest some 'nasty' things to eat such as 'worms on toast', 'fried flies' or 'a boiled slug'. Then go the other way round the circle. This time the children are to request food – for example, 'Please may I have … a sandwich, a yogurt, a banana.'

Rainbow party
- At the rainbow party remind the children of table manners and sharing food. If possible, read a book about good manners (see Resources).

Communication, Language and Literacy

Read a range of familiar and common words and simple sentences independently.

Listening
- Read to the class a story about parties (see Resources).

Writing invitations
- Tell the children that they are going to write invitations for their 'Rainbow party'. Give each of them an A5 piece of paper and write the following in yellow highlighter:
  Dear ____
  Please come to our Rainbow party today at _____o'clock.
  From _____

- Talk about the words and encourage the children to go over the letters with a pencil, fill in the guest's name and the time and end with their names.

High frequency words
- Make two sets of word cards with high frequency words – for example, 'the', 'at', 'my', 'is', 'look', 'help', 'can', 'here', 'I', 'play' and 'you'. Deal one set of the cards, giving each child two cards. Hold up one card from the master set and ask the children to check if they have the matching card. Challenge them to read the word. Continue until each child has matched their words; then go round the circle asking children to read the word in their left hand and their right hand.

Extension
- Bring in a small toy such as a car or a teddy bear. Deal out the cards as above, say a sentence and challenge the children to organise themselves into a 'human sentence' with the words in the correct order and the teddy/car in the right place. For example, 'Here is my teddy.' 'Look at my teddy.' 'Can you help my teddy?' 'Can my teddy play?'

Shared writing
- Explain to the children that you are going to write a sentence about your favourite colour. Orally construct your sentence before writing it (for example, 'I like the colour red best. It is the colour of my front door.') and then discuss the writing process as you write – where to start writing, letter formation and so on. Give each child appropriately coloured paper and invite them to write a sentence based on the model. Display these sentences around the original rainbow picture.

Mathematical Development

Begin to relate addition to combining two groups of objects and subtraction to taking away.

Explore more and less
- Talk about setting the table – for two people, for four people. Ask the children what they would need to do if two more people came to tea. Ask: How many plates would you need? If one person said they could not come, what would you have to take away? How many plates would there be left on the table? Practise number formation on whiteboards.
- Draw a large number line and provide a pile of play foods. Ask a child to find four items and to show you where they

Mixing colours

would go on the number line, counting them as they go. Discuss what you do if you add one more piece of fruit. Talk about where you would land on the number line and where you would be if you took away two pieces of fruit.

Spatial awareness

- Use commercial jigsaws, matching colour and shape. See Resources for useful Internet sites for jigsaws where children can practise rotation and orientation.

Knowledge and Understanding of the World

Find out and identify some objects they observe.

Using coloured lenses

- Create coloured lenses by taping different coloured Cellophane over the end of cardboard tubes. Invite children to study objects through the coloured lenses. What is different? What effect does it have?

Colour games

- Use commercial games (see Resources) to explore colour mixing – for example, 'Colour Paddles'.

Creative Development

Explore colour, texture, shape, form and space.

Painting

- Demonstrate how to drop a blob of paint into a beaker of water. Watch how the colour of the water changes. Encourage the children to describe what they see, using words such as 'pale', 'watery', 'bold', 'shades of colour', 'dark', 'light' and 'bright'.
- Wash over sheets of art paper with a damp cloth. Invite the children to create watery patterns, using only one colour. They should paint a broad band of a dark colour at the top of the page and watch as the paint is absorbed by the damp paper and produces shades of the colour down the page.
- Explore colour mixing – for example, red and yellow = orange; blue and yellow = green; red and blue = purple.

Ask the children what colours might be needed to create brown. Follow their suggestions and discuss the results.

Rainbow biscuits

- Give each child a biscuit and encourage them to decorate it with bands of coloured icing to represent a rainbow. Alternatively, put some icing or jam on the biscuit and sprinkle with hundreds and thousands. Serve the biscuits at the rainbow party.

Rainbow jellies

- Make some red jelly and pour small amounts into clear containers. Leave them to set in the fridge. Make some yellow jelly and leave to cool a while; then carefully pour it over the red jelly in each container. Repeat with other coloured jellies. When set, talk about the layers of colour. Ask: Do they merge? If so, why do you think that happened? Look and record. Serve the jellies at the rainbow party.

Physical Development

Show awareness of space.

Colours game

- Place some strands of coloured wool in the middle of the circle. Give each child a number. Call out a number and a number of coloured strands – for example, 'Number two – two yellow and one blue.' The child who has been allocated that number must run round the circle, back to their own place, then go to the centre and pick up the correct number of coloured strands of wool and bring them to you.

Jelly on the plate

- Sing the song 'Jelly on the plate'. Encourage children to wiggle and wriggle as they say the words 'wibble wobble'.

Review and evaluation

Encourage the children to reflect upon the topic. What have they enjoyed most? Which facts do they remember about the rainbow, colours in the environment and mixing colours? Which artwork did they most enjoy doing?

Starting *with role play – Colour and light*

Poems and songs 1

Diwali morning

There's a rangoli pattern in front of our door,
'Diwali Mubarak' we'll say,
To all our friends and relations
Who will come on this festival day.

I've helped my mum make lots of samosas
And barfi – my favourite sweet.
First we go to the mandir,
Then come back for our festival treat.

When it's evening we'll light up the divas,
They'll twinkle and shine long and bright,
We'll tell tales of how Ram fought Ravana
It's Ram's victory we'll remember tonight.

Jill Bennett

November the fifth

Whizzing, flashing, whirling,
Silver, red and gold.
Catherine wheels and rockets,
Sparklers bright to hold.

Burst of showering fireworks
Fizzing in the sky,
Smoky, crackling bonfire
On top, there's a guy.

Holding baked potatoes
From the fire so red
Now the display's over.
Safely home to bed.

Wendy Lamont

Bonfire night

In the night-time darkness
In the night-time cold,
Did you spot a catherine wheel
Raining showers of gold?
Did you watch a rocket
Go zoom into the sky?
And hear a bonfire crackle
As the sparks lit up the sky?
In the night-time darkness
In the night-time cold
Did you clutch a sparkler
As it scattered stars of gold?

Irene Yates

Candles glowing

(sung to the tune of 'Frère Jacques')

Candles glowing (x2)
In the dark (x2)
Divali is coming (x2)
Celebrate (x2)

Maggie Hutchings

Poems and songs 2

I like colours

I like blue.
I like the sky
Where birds fly high.

I like yellow.
I like the sun
Where we have fun.

I like green.
I like frogs
As still as logs.

I like black.
I like the dark
When foxes bark.

Pie Corbett

I love to row

I love to row in my big blue boat
My big blue boat, my big blue boat:
I love to row in my big blue boat
Out on the deep blue sea.

The big blue boat has two red sails,
Two red sails, two red sails:
My big blue boat has two red sails,
And oars for you and me.

So come and row in my big blue boat,
My big blue boat, my big blue boat:
So come and row in my big blue boat,
Out on the deep blue sea.

What am I hiding?

(To the tune of 'Here we go round the mulberry bush'.)

I am hiding something red,
Something red, something red.
I am hiding something red,
Guess what it can be.

(Do the same with blue, green, yellow, purple and orange.)

Anon

Mixing colours

Mix red and blue for purple,
Mix red and white for pink,
Mix red and black and yellow
And you'll get brown I think.

Why don't you mix some colours?
Mix two or three or four.
You might just mix a colour
No-one's ever mixed before.

Eric Finney

The rainbow house song

(To the tune of 'Here we go round the mulberry bush'.)

Let's go into the Rainbow House,
The Rainbow House, the Rainbow House.
Let's go into the Rainbow House
To see what colour it is.

Today our Rainbow House is red, House is red, House is red.
Today our Rainbow House is red,
Red, red, red.

(Do the same with orange, yellow, green, blue and, in Week 3, purple – indigo and violet.)

The story of Rama and Sita

Once there was a king in India. He had a son called Prince Rama, who married a beautiful princess called Sita. Rama had a wicked step-mother. She did not want Rama to become the next king so she made the king send Rama and Sita into the forest.

Rama and Sita were very happy living in the forest. One day Sita saw a golden deer and she wanted to keep it as a pet, so Rama went off to catch the deer. While Rama was away, Ravana, the wicked ten-headed king, kidnapped Sita and took her back to Lanka, an island far out in the ocean.

When Rama got back he was so upset because his beautiful wife was missing. He asked the monkey army to help him find Sita. They could not find her anywhere. Then a vulture told them that Ravana had stolen Sita and taken her to Lanka. Hanuman, the chief of the monkeys, set off for Lanka to find Sita.

When Sita saw Hanuman she was so happy. 'Please come and rescue me soon,' she said to Hanuman, 'because if I don't agree to marry Ravana, he has said he will eat me up!' Hanuman hurried back to Rama and told him about Sita. Rama collected a great army of monkeys and bears and set off to attack Ravana. Ravana had his best soldiers ready and all day and all night they fought. Then Rama was hit by an arrow. Quick as a flash, Hanuman sped off to find a magic herb which would cure Rama. He was in such a hurry he picked up the whole mountain of herbs and as they dropped to the earth they cured not only Rama but all the other soldiers as well.

Then Ravana, with a helmet on each of his ten heads, raced in his chariot towards Rama. But Rama was ready for him. He put a gold arrow in his bow and fired it. It hit Ravana straight in the heart. The wicked ten-headed king toppled out of his chariot and died. Then there was so much happiness. Sita was rescued by her husband, Rama, and together with Hanuman they rode back home on a great swan. When the people heard they were coming they lit many lamps to welcome Rama and Sita home.

Starting with role play

How to make barfi sweets

Coconut sweets

Ingredients
- 250ml milk
- 500g granulated sugar
- 1 tablespoon butter
- 500g dried milk powder
- 1/2 cup desiccated coconut
- 1/4 cup chopped nuts (almonds and pistachios)

What to do
1. Gently heat the milk in a saucepan. Add the sugar and stir until the mixture comes to the boil.
2. Add the butter, stirring all the time.
3. When the butter has melted, add the coconut and the nuts.
4. Remove the mixture from the heat. Stir in the milk powder.
5. Lightly grease a baking tray. Pour the mixture in and spread it out evenly.
6. Leave the mixture for several hours until it is cold. Then cut it into diamonds or squares.

Diva template and Rangoli design

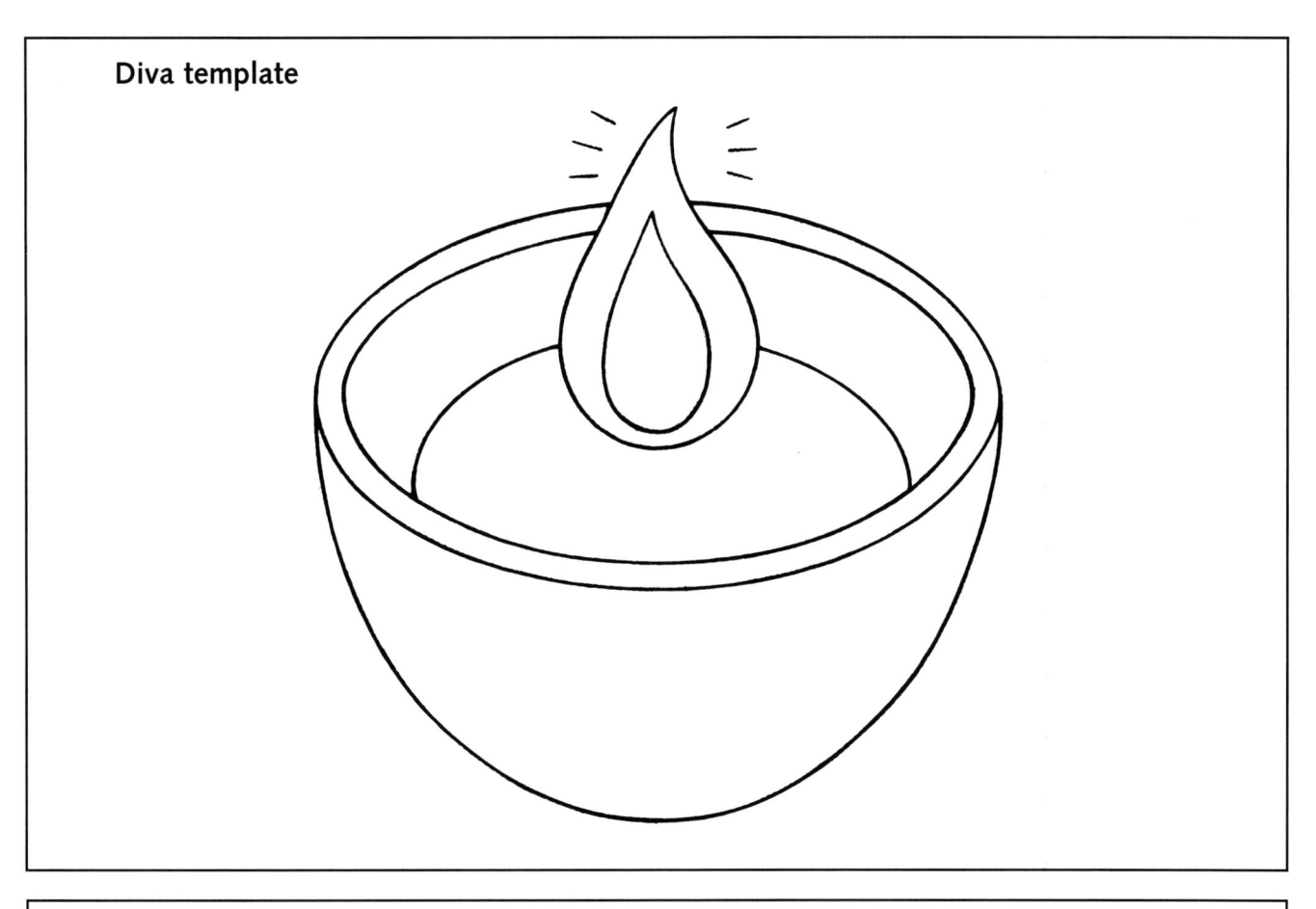

Diva template

Making a rangoli pattern

1. Draw dots, 12 x 12.
2. Join dots in a simple pattern.
3. Colour the pattern.

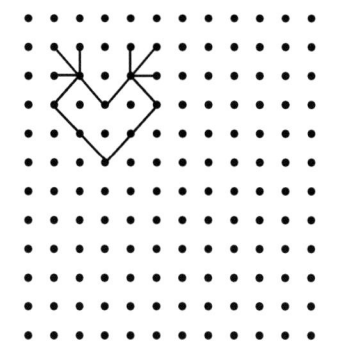

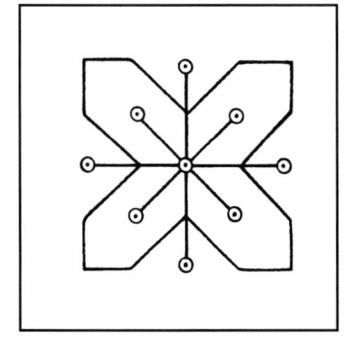

Starting *with role play* 31

Rainbow mobile

32 Starting *with role play*

Template for a periscope

Periscope

You will need
- A tall empty carton (such as a juice carton)
- 2 mirrors wider than the carton
- A triangle of card
- Scissors
- A pen

side *front*

carton

What to do

1. Use the triangle card to draw two diagonal lines, one above the other, on opposite sides of the carton – directly opposite each other. (Figure 1)

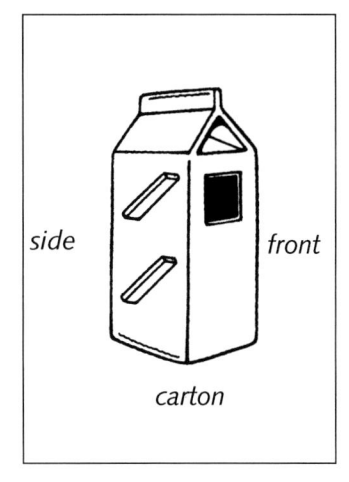

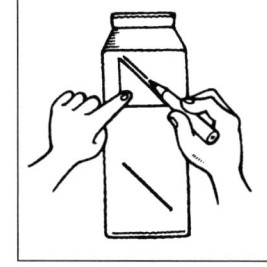

   Figure 1

2. Cut along the lines to make slots wide enough for the mirrors to fit into. Push the mirrors into the slots – the shiny side of the top mirror face downwards; the shiny side of the bottom mirror face upwards. (Figure 2)

   Figure 2

3. Draw a large square on the front of the carton adjacent to the top mirror and cut it out. (Figure 3)

   Figure 3

4. Make a small hole on the back of the carton adjacent to the bottom mirror. Look through the hole to see over the top of obstacles or even round corners. (Figure 4)

   Figure 4

Starting with role play

Template for a kaleidoscope

Kaleidoscope

What you need

- Torch
- Sticky tape
- Beads – different bright colours
- Scissors
- Cards
- Tracing paper
- Three small rectangular mirrors

What to do

1. Tape three mirrors together, shiny sides inwards, to form a triangle. (Figure 1)

Figure 1

2. Draw around the base of the mirrors onto card. (Figure 2)

3. Cut out the triangle of card and make a hole with a pencil in the centre. Tape it to one end of the mirrors.

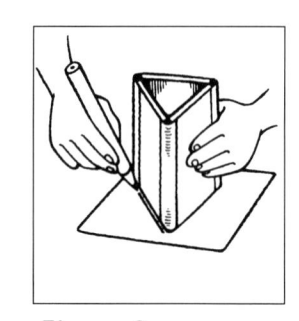

Figure 2

4. Stretch the tracing paper over the other end and attach with sticky tape. (Figure 3)
5. Drop some beads through the hole.
6. Shine a torch into the tracing paper or hold the kaleidoscope up to the light.
7. Look through the hole and see the patterns of the beads. Shake the kaleidoscope and see the change in the patterns.

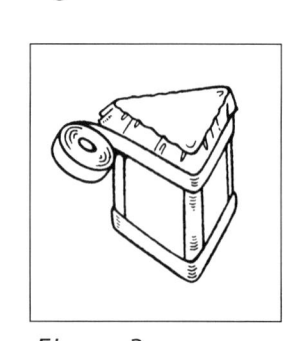

Figure 3

Observational Assessment Chart

Unit: _____   Class: _____   Date: _____

Name	Personal, Social and Emotional Development	Communication, Language and Literacy	Knowledge & Understanding of the World	Mathematical Development	Creative Development	Physical Development
	Y B G ELG	Y B G ELG	Y B G ELG	Y B G ELG	Y B G ELG	Y B G ELG
	Y B G ELG	Y B G ELG	Y B G ELG	Y B G ELG	Y B G ELG	Y B G ELG
	Y B G ELG	Y B G ELG	Y B G ELG	Y B G ELG	Y B G ELG	Y B G ELG
	Y B G ELG	Y B G ELG	Y B G ELG	Y B G ELG	Y B G ELG	Y B G ELG
	Y B G ELG	Y B G ELG	Y B G ELG	Y B G ELG	Y B G ELG	Y B G ELG
	Y B G ELG	Y B G ELG	Y B G ELG	Y B G ELG	Y B G ELG	Y B G ELG
	Y B G ELG	Y B G ELG	Y B G ELG	Y B G ELG	Y B G ELG	Y B G ELG
	Y B G ELG	Y B G ELG	Y B G ELG	Y B G ELG	Y B G ELG	Y B G ELG
	Y B G ELG	Y B G ELG	Y B G ELG	Y B G ELG	Y B G ELG	Y B G ELG
	Y B G ELG	Y B G ELG	Y B G ELG	Y B G ELG	Y B G ELG	Y B G ELG
	Y B G ELG	Y B G ELG	Y B G ELG	Y B G ELG	Y B G ELG	Y B G ELG
	Y B G ELG	Y B G ELG	Y B G ELG	Y B G ELG	Y B G ELG	Y B G ELG
	Y B G ELG	Y B G ELG	Y B G ELG	Y B G ELG	Y B G ELG	Y B G ELG
	Y B G ELG	Y B G ELG	Y B G ELG	Y B G ELG	Y B G ELG	Y B G ELG

Circle the relevant Stepping Stones (Y = Yellow; B = Blue; G = Green or ELG = Early Learning Goal) and write a positive comment as evidence of achievement.

Starting with role play